THE YALE DRAMA SERIES

David Charles Horn Foundation

The Yale Drama Series is funded by the generous support of the David Charles Horn Foundation, established in 2003 by Francine Horn to honor the memory of her husband, David. In keeping with David Horn's lifetime commitment to the written word, the David Charles Horn Foundation commemorates his aspirations and achievements by supporting new initiatives in the literary and dramatic arts.

God Said This

LEAH NANAKO WINKLER

Foreword by Ayad Akhtar

Yale UNIVERSITY PRESS   NEW HAVEN & LONDON

Yale University Press books may be purchased in quantity for educational, business, or promotional use. For information, please e-mail sales.press@yale .edu (U.S. office) or sales@yaleup.co.uk (U.K. office).

Set in Galliard type by Integrated Publishing Solutions, Grand Rapids, Michigan.
Printed in the United States of America.

Library of Congress Control Number: 2019932307
ISBN 978-0-300-24363-5 (paperback : alk. paper)

A catalogue record for this book is available from the British Library.

This paper meets the requirements of ANSI/NISO Z39.48-1992 (Permanence of Paper).

10 9 8 7 6 5 4 3 2 1

Leah: for my mom Ryoko Winkler

Contents

Foreword, *by Ayad Akhtar*   ix

God Said This   1

Foreword

Identity.
A watchword of our time, which can signify both sameness and difference. According to the *Oxford English Dictionary:*

> 1.a The quality or condition of being the same in substance, composition, nature, properties, or in particular qualities under consideration; absolute or essential sameness; oneness.

As well as:

> 2.a The sameness of a person or thing at all times or in all circumstances; the condition or fact that a person or thing is itself and not something else; individuality, personality.

On the one hand, essential sameness; on the other, individuality, or essential difference.

We may descry the unifying thread between these opposing definitions, and still acknowledge the tremendous curiosity that the same word could contain such diametrical valences. Indeed, it is a word whose contrary meanings illuminate the sides of the fundamental divide in our psychological and social lives today.

Are we the same? Or are we different?

In a sense, the questions aren't real. We are both same and different, of course. And in our increasingly politicized era, it falls to the artist—and perhaps only the artist—to show us, to make us see and understand, that both are always true.

God Said This, winner of the 2018 Yale Drama Prize, is about identity in both senses of the word. Leah Nanako Winkler's play depicts a Japanese-American family in Kentucky, but chooses to wear its difference quietly, in service of seeking dramatic union with its audience. In her moving story about a mother's battle with cancer—and the love this process reveals in every member of the family—we can spy the outline of our shared lives as siblings and children and parents. And yes, the unique identities of each of her various protagonists—protagonists, because each of Leah's characters is centrally drawn—are essential, but not in any ultimate sense. *God Said This* is after something more enduring than that.

Before I say more about Leah's play, I think it fitting to say a few words about how it was selected. I took over the judging of this prize from Nicholas Wright in 2018. He inherited from his predecessor, David Hare, a system of empaneling a group to read and assess the more than 1,600 submissions annually. Some of the members of Nicholas's panel stayed on for mine; some members were new. In all, there were twelve of us: writers Dominic Finocchiaro, Susan Stanton, and Annika Boras; directors Matthew Decker, Chris Campbell-Orrock, and Stella-Powell Jones; Niegel Smith, artistic director at the Flea Theatre; Seema Sueko and Natasha Sinha, associate artistic directors at Arena Stage and Lincoln Center/LCT3, respectively; and Ignacia Delgado and Deanie Vallone, literary managers at Sundance Theater Institute and Milwaukee Repertory Theater, respectively. The submissions were divided up and, over a lively five-hour dinner and discussion at the Flea Theatre on a terribly cold downtown December evening, we compiled a short list of twenty-four plays from which the winner and runner-up would end up being selected.

There were plays about oil drilling and corporate malfeasance, about life in a backwoods Appalachian enclave; plays about small-town libraries lending out banned books and about families abandoning civilization for the wide American West. ISIS figured in more than a few stories, and cell phones in the majority of them; dystopian fever-dreams were legion, as were matters of gender, political disaffection, and, of course, love. It was a tantalizing slice of that collective creative consciousness feeding our culture's thoughts and feelings and stories. The breadth and vibrancy of even this slim view was breathtaking.

In *God Said This*, Masako has two daughters and she has cancer. Hiro, her eldest, makes the trip back to Lexington from New York to be by her side, joining the younger daughter, Sophie, and James, her father (and Masako's husband). As in all families, the wounds are both buried and apparent. James's history of alcoholism is a central strand in the family's saga, and it's clear almost from the beginning that Hiro might share some of her father's fateful traits. But we will never know for certain, for the play's compass is magnetized not to trauma but to the love beneath the wounding.

A quirky, hybrid family reunites around the illness of the mother at its center, and in the process, each member of that family comes to experience the love which, despite everything, binds them together inextricably. Not a new story, but Leah's version of it is uncommonly wise. She knows how perfect our parents' flawed love for us can be, and knows, too, that the spectre of death can shape profound human meaning not only in our stories, but in our lives. And so, from the specific condition of a Japanese-American family living and dying in Kentucky—through the witty, poignant estrangement of the familiar in her deft dramatic hands— Leah conveys us to an experience of the universal.

Identity leading to identity.

Plays, of course, are meant to be seen and heard, not read, though a published copy can move through the world as a production cannot, and perhaps in so doing, find that reader whose interest is piqued, who will gather her friends and/or colleagues to give a play its living due.

Encounters with live audiences are what I wish for so many of the wonderful plays that we read this year, and in particular, the runner-up to this year's prize: *Lyons Pride,* by Bleu Beckford-Burrell, a moving play about a Jamaican family in Queens struggling with American life. It's a beautiful story waiting—as of this writing—to be experienced on a stage.

Leah's play has been fortunate to go on to productions at Humana and Primary Stages. Hopefully, there will be many more to come.

Until you can see it yourself, I hope you enjoy it here . . .

Ayad Akhtar

God Said This

God Said This was first produced by Actor's Theater of Louisville's 42nd Humana Festival of New American Plays in February 2018 and subsequently by Primary Stages at the Cherry Lane Theater in January 2019. It was directed by Morgan Gould. The cast was as follows:

JAMES   Jay Patterson

MASAKO   Ako

SOPHIE   Emma Kikue

HIRO   Satomi Blair

JOHN   Tom Coiner

Characters

(3 Females, 2 Males)

JAMES   50s or 60s. A recovering alcoholic. Inappropriate. Can be mean but can be surprisingly sentimental. Seeking redemption but will never say he's sorry. Funny at times but only when he doesn't mean to be. Kentuckian.

MASAKO   50s or 60s, his wife. Has cancer. A total optimist and a beam of light, though when sad the tears cut deep. Masako's resilience is her strength—even if it's not so obvious at first. Japanese immigrant.

SOPHIE   29, their youngest daughter. Kind, patient, but imperfect. Her biggest fears have come to life and she is on the verge of a breaking point. Kentuckian. A born-again Christian.

HIRO   36, their eldest daughter. New York transplant. Isn't always aware of how she affects others but is making a huge effort to be there for her family. Can be cool and collected, but epiphanies hit her all at once to the point of overwhelming emotion.

JOHN   37, Hiro's friend from high school. A funny, straightforward, don't take no shit kind of person. Kind of a jerk actually. But a respectable one. Sometimes has a dark anger behind his eyes. Kentuckian.

Time: 2017

Place: The play takes place over four-ish days—mostly at the
Marky Cancer Center in Lexington, Kentucky. Sometimes
the characters are in cars, hallways, or Alcoholics Anonymous
meetings, but lighting and chairs can indicate the location.

Playwright's Note: James, Masako, Hiro, and Sophie are
meant to be a mixed-race family, and remember that Kentuckian doesn't always mean white. This is also a family who
doesn't know what to do with each other. They don't know
how to love each other, but the love is there. Don't rush
through it. Also, remember that James isn't a hero. He's
done terrible things. Hiro isn't shallow. Sophie's Christianity
isn't a joke. John means everything he says. Masako isn't
weak; she is full of life.

Prologue

In the darkness we hear SOPHIE *and* HIRO *on the phone.*

SOPHIE   I talked to God about Mama.

HIRO   Oh?

SOPHIE   And we can't try. We can't try to fix it. The situation is unfixable. And our mission is simple.

HIRO   Our mission . . .

SOPHIE   Is to make Mama happy. That's what we have to do: make Mama happy. Do you understand?

Act 1
Scene One

DAY 1. Lights up on JAMES. *He's at an AA meeting. He speaks with a Kentucky drawl.*

JAMES   Hi. Well y'all know my fucking name. But I'm James. James Rose. And I am an alcoholic.

(pause)

Today I just wanted to say what I've been thinkin' about. And what I've been thinkin' about is women. Damn women! There was a time in my life when every fucking woman in my life was hard on me. I dunno if they were all on their periods at the same time or what but they were hard on me. My wife. My mother. My daughters— the eldest especially. She never comes 'round, that one. Even when I was sick she never came around. But now that Masako, that's my wife—now that she's sick—she's back. Least for the next few days. Wanted to be with her at the hospital.

(mocking)

Women stick together. Tee hee. Hee.

So, all the women in my life are together again in Kentucky. Well minus my mother. Don't miss her much, may she rest in hell. But every other woman is here. And it's making me wanna. It's making me wanna drink.

I ran away from problems before I was sober. I liked to disappear. I liked to forget everything and have me some fun I couldn't remember. And now? I feel everything! My wife's sickness. I feel that. My eldest daughter's hate—I feel that too. And well—the younger one, she loves Jesus so she don't hate. But I can feel her looking at me with this sympathy which gets to me more, 'cause, well—I don't need nobody feelin' bad for me.

What else?

Oh.

Been tryin' to sell some of my shit down at the flea market. Y'all should come by. I got these cool-ass rocks. I got a Facebook page about it. People seem to like it. Or actually, they do "like" it. Clickity clack.

(pause)

So yeah. That's what I've been thinking about. And I thought I'd let you know.

Scene Two

Same day. Hospital. MASAKO *lies in the hospital bed. She's asleep, wearing a soft cancer specific hat. She's hooked up to medical sensors. There's a chemotherapy drip.* SOPHIE *is on the couch, reading something like* Gone Girl, *and she's riveted. A few beats. Then,* MASAKO *wakes up, unbeknownst to* SOPHIE. *She takes her hat off, scheming. We see her bald head for a brief moment before she puts on another hat—a cute, funny one with two long braids attached. She speaks with a Japanese accent.*

MASAKO   SOPHIE!!!!!! SOPHIE!!!!!!

SOPHIE   *(scared)* WHAT. WHAT. MAMA. WHAT'S WRONG?

MASAKO   . . . My hair growed back.

SOPHIE *sees her mother with the fake braids and laughs.*

SOPHIE   Wooow.

MASAKO   It's miracle!

SOPHIE   With God—anything is possible! Thank you Jesus.

MASAKO   Thank you Jesus!

They laugh.

SOPHIE   Feelin' okay?

MASAKO   Just little nausea.

SOPHIE   Already? The chemo's not started yet on the drip I don't think. Want me to call the nurse?

MASAKO   No, no. I just feel nausea when I come here. It's the thinking about hospital food. Just seeing lady with hospital food I feel nausea automatic.

SOPHIE   Well she isn't very nice.

MASAKO   Colleen.

SOPHIE   Right. Colleen.

MASAKO   See. I say her name right. But she cannot say mine. She call me *Maseiiiko.* And one time, *Yoko!* I can't wait for this be over.

SOPHIE   Well, just think—by Friday—no more chemo!

MASAKO   And no more cancer.

A sad pause. SOPHIE *doesn't respond to this but instead looks at* MASAKO *with worry. Her mother's future is uncertain and the optimism can be heartbreaking.*

MASAKO   Cancer no baka.

SOPHIE   Cancer no baka!
   (pause)
   It's been a long six months of treatment, huh.

MASAKO   Sooo looong.

SOPHIE   They say the last stretch is the toughest but you won't be alone. Not for a second.

MASAKO   I so sorry I worry everyone. Such inconvenience!

SOPHIE   You *love* that everyone's here. You love it.

MASAKO   *(coy)*
Maaaybe.
(pause)
I hope everyone get along!

SOPHIE   Me too. I've been praying on it. Actually let's pray again. Just to make sure.

MASAKO   Okay.

SOPHIE *closes her eyes.* MASAKO *does too, but then opens her eyes about halfway through—watching her daughter with warmth.* MASAKO *isn't a born-again Christian like her daughter—but she likes the idea of God. And she likes making her daughter happy by participating in the ritual of religion.*

SOPHIE   Lord, I feel your strength through the resilience you give us as we fight this horrible disease. Please let us get through the next few days with courage and perseverance and grace. Please help us heal. And Lord, please help our family get along. Please help Hiro have a peaceful time in Kentucky and let her open up her heart to *everyone*—including Dad. And please help Dad continue in his growth and change and thank you for the blessing you gave him in the form of his alcoholism being forced to come to an end through liver failure because too much of something doesn't do anyone no good. Unless of course— it's you, Lord.

(pause)

Oh. And we pray for Colleen. For a woman with such a bad attitude must be suffering in her life with her own struggles. Amen.

MASAKO   Amen.

A pause. They look at each other.

MASAKO   Sophie.

SOPHIE   Yes mama?

MASAKO   Are my eyebrows still on?

SOPHIE   You could use a touch-up.

MASAKO   Give me give me!

SOPHIE   Okay!

SOPHIE *goes to her mother's bag and gets out an eyebrow pencil. She climbs into bed and touches up her mother's hairless eyebrows.*

MASAKO   Yaaay.

Scene Three

Same day. JOHN*'s car.* JOHN *and* HIRO *are driving on a country road.* JOHN *is packing a bowl.* HIRO*'s phone beeps with a text.*

HIRO   Shit, I gotta get back to the hospital soon. Can you pack that a little faster?

JOHN   You do it, then. I'm driving.

HIRO   Fine.

JOHN   You're welcome, by the way, for picking you up and taking you for a dip on these beautiful country roads.
(pause)
Bet you don't have country roads in New York.

HIRO   I summer upstate on the weekends. There are country roads there.

HIRO *packs the bowl. A beat. There is a harsh casualness between her and* JOHN. *They are old acquaintances who have known each other forever without really knowing each other but are familiar anyway. Nothing between them is supersentimental.*

JOHN   So I officiated Laura and Adam's wedding.

HIRO   Yeah I saw the pictures. I *cannot* believe I wasn't invited. I mean, I wouldn't have gone but they should've invited me—

JOHN   —I love officiating weddings actually. I've done like nine. Wanna do more—

HIRO   —How are they doing anyway? Adam and Laura?

JOHN   They got like four kids. Motherfuckers can't pull out of a parking space. And I don't talk to them that much anymore actually. Adam sold his house. Moved the family to Louisville.

HIRO   Louisville makes sense for Laura. But seems too city for Adam.

JOHN   Fuck Louisville. Fuck Rick Pitino. Fuck those flannel-wearin' ghost-huntin' didgeridoo-playin' Louisville fucking hipsters.

HIRO   Hicksters.

JOHN   Hick?

HIRO   Yeah. Like hipsters but with hicks.

JOHN   Haa hickster.
     (genuinely kind of impressed that a woman can be funny)
   That's actually pretty funny. Maybe Lexington's trying to be hickster now too though. They been opening a bunch of gastro pubs and shit.

HIRO   Oh yeah! I read about that on Trip Advisor.

JOHN   *Trip Advisor?* How long has it been since you've been back?

HIRO   My sister's wedding was seven years ago so . . . I guess seven years. And I hadn't come back for seven years before that.

JOHN   How biblical of you.

HIRO   *Why?*

JOHN   Well the Bible shows us that God uses "sevens" throughout the Scriptures to denote prophetic time. Like for example—"Behold, there come seven years of great plenty!"

HIRO   You religious?

JOHN   Not really. I mean I just read a lot.

HIRO   *(genuinely kind of impressed that a man from Kentucky reads)*
Wow.

JOHN   Ugh. Don't be impressed because I *read*, Hiro. That's so "East Coast liberal" of you. There are smart people here and dumb people here. Just like anywhere else.

HIRO   Okay okay.

HIRO *takes hit.*

HIRO   Shit! I forgot how strong Kentucky weed was.

JOHN   It's all from Colorado and California actually.

HIRO   It's such a nice way to get my mind off things.

A beat. He thinks about not asking—but then does.

JOHN   So. How bad is it? Your mom.

HIRO   *(unsentimental)* Pretty bad. She has this thing called carcinosarcoma, which is like this rare and aggressive cancer cocktail that comes from two different types of cells.

JOHN   So she gonna die?

HIRO   It's hard to tell if she'll die soon or like in five years. They cut out the tumor from her uterus a few months ago and now they're pumping her with chemo to try to prevent it from coming back.

JOHN   Jeez.

HIRO   I'm on this Facebook group about it actually because there isn't that much research. But people on it keep dying and it's depressing as fuuuuck. Abigail Vaughn from Minneapolis wrote today: Five weeks ago my mom was diagnosed with carcinosarcoma. This morning she died at the age of fifty-six.

JOHN   *Five weeks?*

HIRO   I guess I'm leaving the group now. Thanks for the support everyone . . . well except for you—@Emilia Parsons. The things you said about "holistic healing" were extremely offensive.

JOHN   Emilia Parsons. What a scrappy hoe.

HIRO   That thread was really stressful. But I like getting information from real people. The truth calms me down even if it's bad. Especially when it comes to illness.

JOHN   Hey isn't your dad sick too? I see him at Chinoe pub a lot singing karaoke and I heard that—

HIRO   He has cirrhosis. It was stage four actually but his liver like healed itself after he quit drinking and now he doesn't have to have a transplant. So unfair.

JOHN   He was pretty shitty right? I remember that like from high school that he was shitty.

HIRO   Yeah he's still shitty. But he's weaker. I'm not scared of him anymore. I feel like I could kill him at any minute if I wanted.
(pause)
You *know*, we were *estranged* for a long time.

JOHN   Estranged? From your dad? Ha-ha that's so entitled.

HIRO   What? Why?

JOHN   Because that's your dad, ya dum-dum.
(pause)
My dad was shit too. He's dead now, though.

HIRO   *(unsentimental)* I remember that. Didn't he pull a gun out on your mom or something?

JOHN   *(unsentimental)* Yeah.

HIRO   *(casual)* How's she doing?

JOHN   *(casual)* Good. Great actually! She retired. She's dating a nice dude. They watch my kid for free so I can smoke weed with you.

HIRO *gives* JOHN *a look.*

JOHN   *I don't do things like this often.* Besides thirteen-year-olds are very independent.

HIRO   OH MY GOD YOUR KID IS THIRTEEN?

JOHN   Um. I'm thirty-seven. That's a relatively normal age to have a thirteen-year-old kid. You weirdo.

HIRO   Who's the mom??

JOHN   This stupid cunt I have to tolerate for the rest of my life.

HIRO   That is VERY disrespectful.

JOHN   Dude. If you knew her—you'd say the same thing. She broke down my door with *my own grand-mother's cast iron cornbread skillet* and bashed me on the head.

HIRO   . . . well what did you do to *make* her do that?

JOHN   I wouldn't let her have my kid when she was high on fucking heroin. Thank God I have primary custody now, but it was scary for a while.
     (pause)
     Anyway I was surprised you contacted me; we were never really that close.

HIRO   Well you're like the only high school person who comments on my Facebook, which means you're the only person I've kept in touch with.

JOHN   That's sad.

HIRO   God you're right. That *is* sad. I'm sad. I'm sad
and old.
   (pause)
   I *had* friends here.

JOHN   I feel you. That's how it goes. There are people
I was close to who I see at Kroger and we say hiiii but it's
weird now.

HIRO   Nicole VanCamp. She was my best friend here.

JOHN   Don't think I saw you at the funeral.

HIRO   You went?

JOHN   Everyone went. That's what friends do.

This kind of stings.

HIRO   If you don't want to hang out with me you don't
have to.

JOHN   I'm the one who asked you to hang. You just
messaged me looking for food recommendations.
   (pause)
   And don't you worry. This is *a hundred percent platonic.*

HIRO   . . . wow you just really had to throw that in
there, didn't you?

JOHN   Well you never know how someone's interpreting
your intentions.

HIRO   But like *a hundred percent platonic? A hundred
percent?*

JOHN   Okay—ninety-nine.

HIRO   I have a boyfriend.

JOHN   Well, we'll go back to a hundred percent again.

They drive.

Scene Four

Same day. Hospital. MASAKO *is asleep.* SOPHIE *is not. Maybe she's on the couch trying to read. She is caught off guard when* JAMES *enters.*

JAMES   Hi ho.

SOPHIE   Dad! What are you doing here?

JAMES   Just felt like comin', I guess.

SOPHIE   Oh. Well, it's not your turn.

JAMES   I know.

SOPHIE   I'm waiting for Hiro to come tag me out.

JAMES   Okeedokie.

SOPHIE *realizes her father is here to stay. She tries to make the best of it.*

SOPHIE   How was AA?

JAMES   Fucking stupid. Went to karaoke afterwards. For a song.

SOPHIE   Yeah? What'd you sing this time?

JAMES *sings a verse of an Elvis song. Perhaps something like* "Heartbreak Hotel."

JAMES   *(speaking)* It's Elvis. That's Elvis.

HIRO *enters carrying a crafty food bag.*

HIRO   Sophie! Mom! I got us fun gastro pub food to eat.
   (seeing JAMES*)*
   What are *you* doing here?

SOPHIE   *Hiro you're late—*

JAMES   —Just felt like comin', I guess—

HIRO   —Mom . . . you awake . . . ?

SOPHIE   Don't wake her!

HIRO   *(to* MASAKO*)*
   Want some . . . Collard Green Kimchi? Or Duck and Waffles?

SOPHIE   *She can't eat today. She doesn't have the appetite.*

HIRO   She should at least have something—

SOPHIE   —She *can't*—

HIRO   That worries me.

JAMES   IT'S FINE.

SOPHIE *and* HIRO *jump. They look to* JAMES *with tension. Is he going to freak out?*

JAMES   Eat when you want. Don't eat when you don't
want. Meal times are a man-made social construct. They're
scam!

He has nothing else to say.

HIRO   . . . 'Kay.

HIRO *sits next to* SOPHIE.

SOPHIE   You reek.

HIRO   Shit, I do?

MASAKO   It's fine.

Everyone looks at MASAKO.

MASAKO   Marijuana is fine. Your father smoke it all the
time. He reek, too. I like it.

HIRO   Hiii Mom!!!!

MASAKO   Hiiii!

HIRO   Sorry! Didn't mean to wake you.

SOPHIE   Yes you did.

MASAKO   It's okay, Sophie. I'm happy. Cancer bring
everyone together.

*Let a few beats go by. This is a family who doesn't know what
to do with each other.* SOPHIE *faintly coughs.* HIRO *stares
blankly ahead.* MASAKO *beams.* JAMES *fiddles on his smart
phone.*

JAMES . . . Well. I took a picture of myself for only the second time in my life yesterday.

HIRO Like a selfie? You took a selfie?

JAMES Yeah.
(pause, this takes a little bit of courage)
I'll show you if you want.

HIRO I thought you hated machines. You literally threw a computer at me once.

JAMES I still don't like the computer. But I like the phone. I got my rock friends on Facebook.

HIRO What do you mean, "rock friends"? Like . . . rock 'n' roll?

SOPHIE No. He collects rocks now. Heaps and heaps of rocks.

JAMES I do.

MASAKO He does.

JAMES *(a huge effort to say this)*
You know, Hiro. Uh. Before you leave. I'd like to sit at a table with you and I'd like to show you my rocks.
(pause, serious)
They're amazing.

HIRO *(prompt but kind)*
No thanks.

MASAKO Hiro, please be nice to your father.

SOPHIE   Yeah, Hiro. Be nice. It'll make everyone
really, really happy. If you go to the house to look at
Dad's rocks.

MASAKO   mmm hmmm!

Everyone looks at HIRO *with great anticipation.*

HIRO   UGH, okay fine. I will come over to look at your
rocks.

JAMES   You will?

SOPHIE   *(to herself)*
    Yes!

JAMES   Good, then. Come by the house in the morning.
I'll pull out the good ones.

JAMES *is very happy. This makes* MASAKO *happy.*

SOPHIE   *(a little frantic)*
    You know Mama . . . Dad. When Hiro comes over to
the house maybe just maybe I can sneak out of here for a
few minutes too? And . . . and she and I can clean? Just a
little teensy bit?

MASAKO   Clean? Clean what?

SOPHIE   Just like maybe the living room and the
kitchen—

MASAKO   —living room kitchen is fine.

SOPHIE   Can we paint, then? *Everything's* peeling—

MASAKO   *I will do it.* I'll clean and paint when I get better. That not your job. Is my job. Plus your father has his things. Right, James?

Everyone looks at JAMES. *He's engrossed in his phone.*

MASAKO   James. JAMES!!!!

JAMES *looks up from his phone, startled.*

JAMES   . . . HUUUUHHHHH?

MASAKO   Never mind. Let me see selfie.

JAMES *shows* MASAKO *his selfie.*

MASAKO   Hyu hyu!!! So handsome. But you should smile more. You are more handsome. When you smile.

A click and maybe a flash! MASAKO *takes a selfie with* JAMES. *She smiles. She is radiant.* JAMES *is blushing, a little caught off guard.*

Scene Five

DAY 2. JAMES *again, at an AA meeting. You get the sense that he enjoys talking to an audience.*

JAMES   Hi again I'm James. James Rose. And I'm an alcoholic blah blah blah. Heh. Heh. Heh. So I don't like movies. Haven't been in years the last one I saw in the theater was *Groundhogs Day.* Didn't like it. But I've been thinkin' a lot this early A.M. about movies because movies have this thing that life don't have a lot of, and that is redemption. Shit, people get redeemed in movies. Crackers get hearts of gold and they are forgiven and they are fixed. I used to think all that was bullshit. But lately I'm thinkin' maybe . . . maybe not.
   (pause)
   I'm not a man who tries to change what he can't control. But I can control myself, when I try very, very hard. And so today I will participate in Serenity.
   (maybe closing his eyes, maybe not)
   God grant me the serenity to accept the things I cannot change;
   Courage to change the things I can;
   And wisdom to know the difference.
   Living one day at a time;
   Enjoying one moment at a time;
   Accepting hardships as the pathway to peace;
   (pause)
   Oh guess what y'all? My daughter. The eldest one who hates my guts. She's coming over to the house this morning! She's coming to see my rocks!

Scene Six

Same Day. Hospital. SOPHIE *is pacing around. She is pissed.* HIRO *enters, clearly hungover.*

HIRO   . . . hey.

SOPHIE   *(aggressive whisper)*
Hiro. Hallway! Now!

SOPHIE *drags* HIRO *into the hallway.*

SOPHIE   *Out drinking all night?*

HIRO   . . . so?

SOPHIE   So?!?! SO?!?!? You were supposed to meet Dad at the house this morning to look at his rocks!!!!!

HIRO   *(not bratty, genuine)*
Oh. Shit I forgot.

SOPHIE   Let me guess. *Because you were with some guy?*

HIRO   . . . yeah. But it's a hundred percent platonic!

SOPHIE   *I call a hundred percent bullshit!*

A moment. SOPHIE *and* HIRO *both gasp, they are shocked that* SOPHIE *said a curse word. Because of her religion it's been years since* SOPHIE *has cursed. She covers her mouth.*

HIRO   Oh my God Sophie Leonore Rose Williams. You
cursed!!! You cursed with your mouth! I'm texting your
husband *right now!*
    (on her phone)
    Dear Da'Ran, you will never guess what sin your perfect
little born-again Christian wife committed devil emoji
devil emoji devil emoji devil emo—

SOPHIE *grabs* HIRO*'s phone out of her hand and throws it on
the ground. Hard.* HIRO *is taken aback.*

SOPHIE   It's not funny!!!!!! None of this is funny. Don't
you understand that it's not funny!!?!?!?

HIRO   *(genuine)*
    I'm . . . sorry. Sophie, I'm sorry.

SOPHIE *is really upset.* HIRO *takes this in.*

SOPHIE   I *really, really* wish you would have went to
the house, Hiro. I wanted you to see what condition it's
in. *I needed you to.*

HIRO   It's that bad?

SOPHIE   *Everything* is falling apart. And on top of that,
Dad's *such* a hoarder.

HIRO   *(trying to be helpful)*
    Well that's not surprising. Grandma was a hoarder.
Grandpa was a hoarder. We come from a family of hoarders.
This is why I throw everything away even gifts and day-old
food, with no sense of remorse—

SOPHIE   —and he can't take care of himself. Mama did
everything. And now that she's not strong enough there's

piles of dirty clothes and underwear just everywhere. And dishes. Dust rising up from the furniture. Black mold in the bathroom. Clutter on top of clutter. But I can't do anything about it because it just upsets Mama and now Dad's gonna come back and he's gonna be mad because you didn't see his rocks and Mama shouldn't be around that kind of energy right now!!!!! GOD HIRO. WHY DIDN'T YOU LOOK AT HIS ROCKS?!?!! WHY HIRO WHY?

HIRO   I dunno I just. I'll go *now*. Okay? I'll go now.

SOPHIE   Well you can't go NOW. *I* have to go to work and you have to stay with Mama.

HIRO   Can't you call in?

SOPHIE   I don't get paid if I'm not there. And we need the money.

HIRO   Hey! Between your church and me we've been covering a lot of it. Remember—I'm an account director now with like assistants and everything!

SOPHIE   *It's more than you think.*

HIRO   I *make* more than you think.

SOPHIE   Well the chemo's only partially covered and the scans are covered every six months for the first year and then only once a year after that. But she needs to get one at least every three months for the rest of her life so you'll pay that out of pocket?

HIRO   Well—according to the *carcinosarcoma Facebook group*—

SOPHIE   I hate the carcinosarcoma Facebook group,
Hiro! I wish you wouldn't have added me.

HIRO   But we can't just blindly trust everything the
doctors say! The fucking health care in this fucking country is—

SOPHIE   Not right now.
   (pause)
   Hiro, remember what I said to you before you came
back? Remember the mission I gave you?

HIRO   To make Mom happy.

SOPHIE   So please. Get your stuff together!

SOPHIE *heads out.*

HIRO   Okay bye I love you! SOPHIE I LOVE YOU.

SOPHIE *stops. Turns. Looks at* HIRO.

SOPHIE   Then why do you always need a man around?

HIRO *is taken aback.*

HIRO   I don't always need a—

SOPHIE   Hiro, you're so strong and independent and
I love that about you. But at home—you always, *always*
need a man around. Why?

HIRO   That is *so* not true—

SOPHIE   —uhm yes it is. You brought that Adam guy
to my wedding last-minute. And in high school you were

always hanging out with your twenty-two-year-old boy-
friends from Hot Topic.

HIRO   Tilford was eighteen and Blaze was *barely* twenty
but okay—

SOPHIE   It's like you can't just *be here*. Well guess what,
Hiro? Now is the time to just *be here*.

SOPHIE *exits. A beat.* HIRO *takes a moment. Then she salvages
her phone. It still works. She sends a text. She heads to the
hospital room.* MASAKO *is awake.*

MASAKO   Hiro chan. I made you oinari san. It's in mini-
fridge. So nice there is mini-fridge. So luxurious. Like nice
hotel.

HIRO   Mom—you shouldn't have.

MASAKO   You love oinari san.

HIRO   You should be resting.

MASAKO   All I do is resting.

HIRO   No, I mean. You should have been resting *before*
chemo started up again. You don't know how to—
    (catching herself)
Never mind. Sorry.
    (pause)
I mean.
Thank you.

MASAKO   Eat.

HIRO *eats.*

MASAKO   Oishii?

HIRO   Oishii. Want some?

MASAKO   Everything tastes bad.

HIRO   Do you want some water?

MASAKO   Water tastes bad.

HIRO   Do you wanna watch a movie?

MASAKO   Movies are bad. Last one I saw in movie
theater was *Groundhog Day.*
   I did not like.

HIRO   Then uhhh.
   Do you wanna like. Tell me your life story?

MASAKO   . . . what?

HIRO   You know. You can tell me your life story. And I
can like, get to know you all over again and stuff. What
was your earliest memory?

JAMES   *I waited for you this morning!!!*

*JAMES has entered. He's carrying a very large garbage bag
and looks livid.*

JAMES   I waited for you this morning because you were
supposed to look at my rocks! But you didn't show up!

He breathes heavily. HIRO *and* JAMES *make eye contact. A
beat.*

JAMES   So. I brought some of my rocks to you!!!

JAMES *slams the heavy bag on the ground.* HIRO *jumps.*
*Then—*JAMES *begins taking some rocks out of the garbage
bag, still livid.*

JAMES   These are. These are some of my *favorites.* You
can pick one out. And take it back to New York. If you
want.

MASAKO   Ooooh how nice, James. *Pick a rock* Hiro *chan.*

JAMES   Yeah pick one.

MASAKO   *(abrasively to* HIRO*)*
     Pick one.

JAMES   Any which one you want!

MASAKO   *(kindly to* JAMES*)*
     Can't wait to see what she will pick!

HIRO *looks at her dad, then at her mom, who is looking at her
with great anticipation.*

HIRO   Okay.

HIRO *quickly picks out a random rock.*

HIRO   I'll take this one.

JAMES   OH SHIT!!!!!!! The JASPER INDONESIA.
DIDN'T MEAN TO PUT THAT ONE IN THERE.
     (pause)
     Pick a different one.

HIRO   *(irritated)*
   No.

JAMES   *(aggressive)*
   JUST PICK A DIFFERENT ONE.

HIRO   *(highly aggressive back)*
   NO!

JAMES   DON'T BE SPOILT!

HIRO   HOW THE FUCK AM I SPOILT WHEN I
DID EVERYTHING MY FUCKING SELF MY ENTIRE
LIFE.

JAMES   THAT IS A CROCK OF SHIT. HERE. JUST
TAKE THE HARLEQUIN QUARTZ.

HIRO   I DON'T WANT THE HARLEQUIN
QUARTZ. I DON'T EVEN KNOW WHAT IT IS.

JAMES   THE HARLEQUIN QUARTZ IS A CRYSTAL
INCLUDED WITH THE LEPIDOCROCITE FAMILY.
OFTEN THE INCLUSIONS APPEAR AS TINY RED
STARS OR CLOUDS WITHIN THE TERMINATION
END OF A QUARTZ POINT. IT'S A REMOVER SAID
TO BE A POWERFUL EMOTIONAL BALANCER
OKAY? ENCOURAGING SELF-LOVE. SELF-WORTH
AND HEALING OF OLD SELF-PUNISHING
WOUNDS!!!!

HIRO   I GOT PLENTY OF SELF-LOVE AND SELF-
WORTH AND I WANT THE INDONESIAN WHAT-
EVER IT'S PRETTIER.

JAMES   WELL YOU CAN'T HAVE IT. IT'S TOO
RARE TOO BEAUTIFUL AND YOU DON'T EVEN
KNOW NOTHIN' ABOUT IT!

HIRO, *mad as hell, takes a small bottle of bourbon out of her
purse. She drinks, not breaking eye contact with* JAMES. *She
breathes out, making a lion's breath.* JAMES *can smell the
liquor. He wants it. This is a very tense moment. They don't
break eye contact.*

MASAKO   GOLDFISH!

A beat.

HIRO   What?

MASAKO *is trying to diffuse the situation with positivity.*

MASAKO   My earliest memory is goldfish. Sunbeam
in goldfish bowl. I named goldfish Toon Chan. After
toonkigou. (pause) Toonkigou. Do you know what that
means?

HIRO/JAMES   Treble clef.

MASAKO   Treble clef. That's right. I study music in
Shimabara. Opera. Piano. Flute. I teach songs to pre-
school kids in small country. Then five years after study
I thought—there must be more melody to life I haven't
heard. And that's when I went to America. And I met you.
James. I met you.
   (pause)
And then you came along Hiro chan.

Then, MASAKO *starts dry-heaving.* JAMES *brings her a nearby
barf bowl. She pukes what she can into it.*

MASAKO   I've always loved music.

HIRO *pats* MASAKO*'s head. So does* JAMES. *They stand there like that, patting the head of the woman they both love in a brief united moment. As we seamlessly transition into* . . .

Scene Seven

SOPHIE *stands alone.*

SOPHIE   *(singing)*
    Abide with me; fast falls the eventide;
    The darkness deepens; Lord with me abide.
    When other helpers fail and comforts flee,
    Help of the helpless, O abide with me.
    Swift to its close ebbs out life's little day;
    Earth's joys grow dim; its glories pass away;
    Change and decay in all around I see;
    O Thou who changest not, abide with me.
    Not a brief glance I beg, a passing word,
    But as Thou dwell'st with Thy disciples, Lord,
    Familiar, condescending, patient, free.
    Come not to sojourn, but abide with me.
    (speaking)
    Oh sorry. Welcome to Men's Wearhouse.
    You're going to like the way you look. I guarantee it!
    (pause)
    Oh hi, Travis! How are you? How's the baby? Come on
'round back—I got some awesome suits I wanna show ya!

Scene Eight

JOHN and HIRO get into JOHN's car. They're drunk.

HIRO You sure you're okay to drive? You've had a couple.

JOHN Yeah yeah.

HIRO You sure you sure? Everyone drives drunk in Kentucky and they like die.

JOHN I wouldn't do that to my kid.

He starts the car. Then stops it.

JOHN Okay no you're right. I should wait a little.

HIRO Should I order us a Lyft?

JOHN Nah. Let's just sit here for a second.

HIRO Okay.

A beat. HIRO tries to make out with JOHN.

JOHN Woah woah woah. What are you doing?!?!!?

HIRO Umm. Making out with you?

JOHN   You said you had a boyfriend!

HIRO   I lied.

JOHN   *Why would you lie about that?*

HIRO   Because you said we were a hundred percent
platonic and I was like—how dare he?

JOHN   Well I meant it.

HIRO   Wow. Okay.
    (pause)
    I don't understand why you'd want to hang out with
me, then.

JOHN   Um. Because I'm genuinely interested in people?
Not all men are so single-minded, Hiro. I just wanted to
hang out with you. As a friend. I just want . . . I just want
a connection with a new person. Is that a crime? *Fucking*
isn't what I want from you at all.

HIRO   Who said I wanted to fuck? I just wanted to kiss.
I'm lonely. It's lonely. I get so lonely here by myself with
my family.

JOHN   Okay but Hiro. Do you know how many girls
I've already kissed this week?

HIRO   Uhhh.

JOHN   Three. And we did more than kiss. We fucked.
God I'm so tired!!! I've already fucked three different girls
this week!

HIRO   *You?*
    . . . were they pretty?

JOHN   Oh my God!

HIRO   Sorry. That was rude.

JOHN   Yes. Yes it was!

HIRO   But seriously—were they?

JOHN *chuckles.*

JOHN   Hiro, Hiro, Hiro. You *know* I have a master's
degree right?

HIRO   Yes. From Eastern Kentucky University.

JOHN   *(a college cheer)* EKU WUT WUT?!?! GOOOOO
Colonels!

HIRO   You've told me like a bunch of times.

JOHN   Because it's amazing. Seriously. Do you know
how amazing it is? That I have a fucking master's degree?
Bitches love that shit! On top of that I have a good job.
A nice car! And an adorable son I can take care of and
support while still having a moderate amount of disposable
income! Fuck! I'm a fucking yuppie. Me. A YUPPIE.
That's fucking incredible considering how bad I used
to be!

HIRO   Were you really that bad though?

JOHN   YES.

HIRO   I thought you were just normal bad for like
public school. Like you got arrested for shoplifting at the
Liquor Barn or something.

JOHN   Haaaa oh yeah. And I had to hide my weed in the grid of Justin's truck.

HIRO   Justin Alden, right? From the private school?

JOHN   Lexington Catholic wannabe gangster Justin. See—I was really good at shoplifting. I was slick but that rich bitch motherfucker—he was HORRIBLE at shoplifting! Just like—an untalented bridge troll. Went to the bathroom with an entire case of beer, hid it under his shirt and tried to walk out. It was his fault we got arrested not mine.

HIRO   'Kay.

JOHN   And you know what? I got arrested see—and people at our school were like "Oh, whatever, people get arrested all the time." But JUSTIN gets arrested and he goes back to that SIXTEEN-K-a-year classroom a fucking legend. People thought he was hard as fuck!

HIRO   Hey is Justin Alden still around?

JOHN   Yeah.

HIRO   Is he still uh . . . hot? Cuz if you don't wanna make out with me maybe he will.

JOHN   Oh my God. You don't remember the car accident. Do you?

HIRO *does not.*

JOHN   We were driving in Irvine late one night smoking weed back in the day. I was drunk. Justin was going fast. Couldn't even see the fences painted black over the green.

We started blasting Master P. I don't remember anything
past that but Justin crashed into a tree. Told me he said
John . . . John . . . you okay man? John? And I didn't
answer. So he figured I died. Then he realized his face was
smashed through the windshield. So he pried his face off
the glass and blood was leaking out of his cheeks and his
neck and he just knew he was going to die. So he went to
lay down in the middle of the road, looking up at the stars
and sayin' God—please tell John I'm sorry. Tell my mama
I love her. I'm dead. I'm dead I'm fucking dead. I'm sorry
I'm sorry I'm sorry. I'm sorry.
(pause)
But he ended up being okay. His face is just really
fucked up.

HIRO   Oh my God. How fucked up?

JOHN *shows* HIRO *a picture on his phone.*

HIRO   Holy shit.

JOHN   Anyway, he just kind of went downhill from
there. Kinda sits at home all day. He's on disability not
for his face but because of anxiety.

HIRO   You can get on disability for anxiety?

JOHN   Yeah and he's a former addict. Or an addict.
Depends on the year. Kind of a recluse.

HIRO   God. Sounds like he really fucked up his life.

JOHN   It's really easy to fuck up your life. Like. Really
easy. If I wanted to fuck up my life I could do it right now.
But you know what's hard? *Getting your shit together and
getting a fucking master's degree.*

(pause)

God If I didn't have my kid, I don't know what
would've happened to me. He's the love of my life. When
he turns eighteen, I have to find something else to live for.
But for now, he's what I'm living for.

HIRO   *(genuine, worried about driving drunk in a
real way)*

Give me your keys. I'm ordering us a Lyft.

Scene Nine

Hospital. Same day. JAMES *and* MASAKO *are asleep.* MASAKO *in bed and* JAMES *on the couch or a chair. Then all of a sudden the chemotherapy drip starts beeping. It beeps for quite a while before it wakes* JAMES *up.*

JAMES   Masako?

MASAKO   Mmm.

JAMES   Is that thing beepin'? Or is it my hearing aid?

MASAKO   Thing beeping. But it's okay. Beeping normal.

JAMES   *Well can you tell it to be quiet?*

MASAKO   It will stop. You be patient.

The beeping goes on for a while. Then stops.

MASAKO   See? I professional now.

JAMES   WHAT?

MASAKO   PROFESSIONAL.

JAMES   HUH?

MASAKO   AT CANCER. I PROFESSIONAL.

JAMES   WHAT?

MASAKO   WHAT TIME IS IT.

JAMES   GOT PLENTY OF TIME.

MASAKO   YOU HEARING AID STUCK. COME
HERE.
  (gesturing)
Come come.

JAMES *goes to* MASAKO. *She fixes his hearing aid.*

MASAKO   Better?

JAMES   I was hearing you! It just wasn't . . . clear. Didn't
mean to fall asleep. It must have moved around when I
was lying down.

MASAKO   What time is it?

JAMES   Nighttime.

MASAKO   Mmm. You like nighttime.

JAMES   When it's dark your imagination can start.

MASAKO   I do not like dark.

JAMES   I know it.

MASAKO   But sometime the sun and the moon are together. This side sun and this side moon. And some little
stars. I like that.

JAMES   Play of Light.
(pause)
That's next month's theme in my Facebook group.
"Play of Light."

MASAKO   In rocks?

JAMES   No that's my Facebook page. But I'm also in
some groups. Rocks sure. But light too. And one about
birds. I'm the boss of that one.

MASAKO   *(impressed)*
You are???

JAMES   I get to choose the pictures *and* the covers.

MASAKO   You made it???

JAMES   I didn't *make it*; the guy *stuck me in there.*

MASAKO   What guy?!?!? New friend??

JAMES   Guess so.

MASAKO   And you boss???

JAMES   I didn't ASK for it. But yeah he made me boss.

MASAKO   So cool!!!

JAMES   Yup.

MASAKO   I'm glad you enjoying machines.

JAMES   I told y'all. I really still don't like the computer.
I just like my phone.

MASAKO   That's same thing.

JAMES   No it's not.

MASAKO   Yes it is.

JAMES   It's not sitting at a desk.

MASAKO   But phone is tiny computer.

JAMES   I couldn't sit at a desk for so long! The little
screen I can handle.

MASAKO   I happy for you James. You find joy of internet. You were late to party but you join the party.

JAMES   Ha!

MASAKO   It's fun. I listen and read many stories from
internet. I read about sickness.

JAMES   *Why?*

MASAKO   Because everybody gets sick. And many
people want to talk loudly about it. And I have an internet friend too. Her name Priscilla. She a wild woman. In
Nevada. She been living with for seven years same cancer
as me. She give me hope.

JAMES   How'd you find her?

MASAKO   Popular blog. Every single day she post about
adventures. About treatment. About life. I try to read.

JAMES   What's it called?

MASAKO   "Tumor Has It."

JAMES   Heh. That's pretty good.

MASAKO   James. Will you read me last two days? My
brain Swiss cheese, I have not checked. She getting the
result of her scan soon. I want to know result too.

JAMES   Yeah. I can do that.

Lights up on SOPHIE *sitting alone in her car—also reading
on her phone. She's on the Carcinosarcoma Facebook Group—
upset but unable to look away.*

Then somewhere else—lights up on HIRO *wearing workout
clothes. She's going for a moonlight run.*

HIRO   *(to herself)*
What are you living for?

Then—she sprints. HIRO *sprints in place throughout the entire
duration of the scene, escalating in speed toward the end. She
should be isolated in space with lighting. The idea is that she
is running, feeling her functioning body and taking out her
fear and anxiety through physical exercise to the point of
exhaustion. This scene is a cacophony. It must be fast-paced
and rhythmic.* SOPHIE *and* JAMES *are both reading from their
respective phones but please note they are reading different
content on separate websites.*

JAMES   *(reading from his phone)*
"Tumor Has It. April 13th"

SOPHIE   *(reading from her phone)*
"Carcinosarcoma Facebook Group. April 13th. Lucy
Jones from London."

JAMES "Hey y'all it's Priscilla. Blogdiggity bloggin'
from the Grand Canyon!"

SOPHIE "To say this group has been a lifeline would
be an understatement. Thank you from the bottom of my
heart for your support these past six months."

JAMES "No I'm NOT on my Mac my darlings—I'm not
THAT addicted to technology. I'll publish this ish later at
the Yavapai Lodge."

SOPHIE "So it breaks my heart to post an update that I
knew was coming but still somehow hoped I'd never, ever
have to write."

JAMES "Right now I'm scribblin' in the sunshine on a
notebook littered with bumper stickers from Gotcancer
.org—thanks for the rec Lympho Bob. My favorite? The
one that says CCKMA: CANCER CAN KISS MY ASS!!!!!"

MASAKO Cancer can kiss my ass!!!!!

JAMES "Just yelled that into the cavernous valleys."

MASAKO CANCER CAN KISS MY ASS!!!!!!!

SOPHIE "My mum died. My strong, beautiful and
irreplaceable mum. She died. It happened this morning
at 8:05 UK time."

JAMES "And my voice echoed like a vast angry God."

SOPHIE "I don't know what she did to deserve this
pain."

JAMES "I just feel so much up here."

SOPHIE   "Her body—"

JAMES   "My body."

SOPHIE   "Her poor body."

JAMES   "My strong body."

SOPHIE   "Wasn't a body anymore."

JAMES   "It brings tears to my eyes."

SOPHIE   "It brings tears to my eyes—"

JAMES   "Thinking about what hell my body went through. So I'll share with you something that helped me during times of sadness."

SOPHIE   "I'm just so sad. But I guess. I guess."

SOPHIE/JAMES   "But I feel sad, then I am still alive."

JAMES   "Repeat it out loud."

SOPHIE   "I am alive. I am alive. I am alive. And that means I have to live. I have to live for her."

SOPHIE *puts her phone down, overwhelmed. She wishes she hadn't read that.*

JAMES   "Getting the results from my scan tomorrow. Think of me. Xoxo. Priscilla."

SOPHIE *starts her car, almost in a trance.*

JAMES   "Tumor Has It. April 14th"

(getting caught up in his own reading)
"As you know, I got the results of my scan today. I can't
believe how fast this happened. The beast snuck up and
spread to my lungs"—Oh SHIT.

JAMES *stops himself. He looks over at* MASAKO, *who seems to be
asleep. God please be asleep. He didn't want her to hear that.*

JAMES   Masako, you didn't hear none of that. Did you?
Masako are you alright?

No answer from MASAKO. *Meanwhile,* SOPHIE *is driving fast.
Too fast.*

SOPHIE   I am alive I am alive I am alive I am alive I am
alive I am alive I am alive I am alive I am alive I am—

*Then she gasps—seeing something coming toward her. She
tries to swerve but it's too late.*

*Then bright flashing lights. Crashing sounds. Blackout on
everyone except for* HIRO—*who stops running. She's out of
breath. She breathes in and out. In and out.*

And then we hear MASAKO *crying in the darkness—then
full-on wailing.*

The lights slowly fade in on MASAKO'S *face as she wails and
wails for Priscilla. For her own life.*

HIRO *doesn't see or hear it. She keeps on taking in the Kentucky air. Breathing.*

Breathing. Breathing. Blackout.

END OF ACT 1

Act 2
Scene One

Darkness. A ringing of a phone. It rings and rings and rings and then—

HIRO   *(groggy)* Sophie?

SOPHIE   *(upset)* Hiro.

HIRO   What's wrong? Is mom—

SOPHIE   *I totaled my car.*

The lights gradually come up on HIRO *and* SOPHIE *in separate places. It's early, early morning of Day 3 —before daybreak.*

HIRO   How?

SOPHIE   A deer. I hit it. I hit a friggin' deer because I was so upset at that stupid carcinosarcoma group you added me to on Facebook. Unadd me!!! Unadd me now!!!!

HIRO   That's . . . not how Facebook groups work. You just leave the group on your own accord.

SOPHIE   This is YOUR fault.

HIRO   That's . . . really unfair.
   (pause)
   Are you alright?

SOPHIE   NO. But yes. I only sprained my wrist. But don't you DARE tell Mama about this. It'll just stress her out!

HIRO   I won't.
   (pause)
   Do you need me to come get you?

SOPHIE   I'm with my husband, Hiro. OBVIOUSLY.

HIRO   Hi Da'Ran . . .

SOPHIE   He *doesn't* say hi back.

HIRO   . . . Do you need anything? From me?

SOPHIE   I need you to unadd me from that group. It was mean of you to add me. So, so mean. All those people dying. All those people losing their mothers. I don't need to see that. *I don't need to see that.*

HIRO   Okay. Okay. *(genuine)* I'm sorry. I'm sorry.

SOPHIE   The deer.

HIRO   Hm?

SOPHIE   I had to watch that deer die. On the side of your road—

HIRO   The deer—

SOPHIE   She was lying there after I hit her—all bloody and scared. Her eyes were open. Her small black eyes just filled with death. And she was moving. Moving, Hiro! Her breath pounding against the ground. And her legs . . .

her legs. At first I thought they were twitching but then
I realized . . . she thought she was running, Hiro! She
couldn't even stand but she thought she was running . . .
running away from me. She didn't know she was dying
Hiro! She didn't know she was dying!

Scene Two

DAY 3. JAMES *enters. He's at AA again.*

JAMES   Good mornin'. Hi. Guess who's back again? Me.
It's me. I'm back. Heh.
   (pause)
   Just sucked down some macaroni and cheese. It's hard
when your wife don't cook for ya.
   Forgot to put the butter in. And we didn't have no
milk. So, I put in some mayonnaise.
   Still sucked it down but wasn't as good. Sticky.
   (pause)
   Reachin' the homestretch of chemo. Doctors said the
drip might be done tomorrow morning. Might be the
middle of the night. Hopin' for the middle of the night.
Then—we just wait. Wait in the uncertainty. No. Live in
the uncertainty.
   People hate uncertainty. Drives some people mad.
Which is funny 'cause everything in life is uncertain. Well.
'Cept for death.
   My daughter—the one who hates me—she done shoved
a drink in my face the other day! And shit. I wanted a swig
so badly. It never goes away. Wanting to take a swig. But
God. In that moment I thought about how anger manifests when yer sober and how it manifests when yer not.
   I say—anger sure as hell manifested inside my body
when I was drinkin' I'll tell ya that. I was stupid. Fuckin'
stupid. Didn't think beer was bad for ya. And still don't
think it is. But drink a twenty pack of anything every day

for twenty years and then . . . 'course it's bad. Again, I was stupid. And my body became angry at the stupid. My liver got stiff and lumpy. My skin turned yellow. And my belly— well it swoll out to here until I exploded and I bled out my mouth and ass. Oh and I couldn't walk no more. I remember all I wanted was to be able to walk. I told Masako—I want to walk! I want to walk goddamnit, I want to walk!

And now—by some sort of miracle. I'm walking again. And I don't take it for granted.

(pause)

Nowadays when I feel angry I remember that I can walk. And the anger subsides. It really does.

(pause)

Hi I'm James. And I am an alcoholic.

Scene Three

Hospital. MASAKO *is asleep. She looks five times worse than she did the day before.*

SOPHIE *enters. She's wearing a bandage on her wrist. She looks disheveled, exhausted. She looks at her mom. A beat.*

MASAKO   *(weakly)* tou.

SOPHIE   *(softening)* Mama.

MASAKO   . . . arigatou. Otousan arigatou.

SOPHIE   You dreamin' mama?

MASAKO   *(can barely talk)*
You. Hiro chan. Little girls. Eating candy your papa got from Kroger. Candy . . . make you so happy. You smile so big and you say "Otousan arigatou."

SOPHIE *puts on a long-sleeved sweater—hiding her wrist.*

SOPHIE   I saw Colleen on the way in. She said she tried to come by and take your breakfast order but you turned her away. Still can't eat?

MASAKO   Mmm.

SOPHIE   Feelin' nauseous?

MASAKO   Mmm.

SOPHIE   Do you want me to call the nurse for some
Ativan?

MASAKO   No. Makes me not poo. I want to poo. I miss
the poo.

SOPHIE   Do you wanna go to the bathroom and try?

MASAKO   Mmm.

SOPHIE *helps* MASAKO *out of bed, careful about her wrist. This
is difficult but methodical.* MASAKO *drags her chemotherapy
drip with her. The cord gets caught.*

MASAKO   Close the door.

SOPHIE   It's the cord.

MASAKO   Please close door!

SOPHIE   It's the dang cord!

SOPHIE *releases the cord and tries to help her mother to the
bathroom.*

MASAKO   What you do??

SOPHIE   You're so weak today Ma—

MASAKO   Stop! I said stop!!!! Go away! Go away go
away!!! I can do myself!!!

Then, MASAKO *starts to dry-heave. Sophie rushes to get the
puke bowl. Masako dry-heaves into the puke bowl. This goes*

on for an uncomfortable period of time. MASAKO *then nearly crumbles. She's pissed herself.* SOPHIE *helps* MASAKO *back to bed, slowly. Carefully. Once she's in,* SOPHIE *rushes back to quickly clean the floor with wipes. She then cleans her hands with hand sanitizer. She helps* MASAKO *take off her soiled underwear. This is difficult but methodical. She's done this before.*

MASAKO   I wish time go by faster. I want it to be tomorrow now!!!
    (pause)
    I need new pantsu.

SOPHIE   Yup. Mmm hmm!

SOPHIE *reaches into a bag and gets out a fresh new pair of underwear. She puts it on* MASAKO. *It's clear she's also done this before. A beat.*

SOPHIE   Wanna listen to a sermon on your phone?

MASAKO   No. You can tell me. What God said.

SOPHIE   Me?

MASAKO   You.

SOPHIE   Okay. God said, "As your days, so shall your strength be."
    God said, "My words are life to you."
    God said, "To your old age and gray hairs I will carry you.
    I will deliver you, I will preserve you I will keep you alive.
    I will satisfy you with long life.
    I heal all your diseases and your broken heart.
    I'll bind up your wounds and your light shall break forth

as the morning," God said—
"Your health shall spring forth speedily,"
God said—
"Trusting Me brings health to your navel,"
God said—
"and marrow to your bones,"
God said—
"My joy is your strength.
I will recover you.
I'll make you to live.
I am ready to save you."
And God said this, Mama.
I love you.
Mama, I love you.

Scene Four

Car. JOHN *and* HIRO, *same day, afternoon.* JOHN *seems weird.*

HIRO   That barbecue was good.
(pause)
Thanks for calling me on your lunch break and taking me to barbecue.
(pause)
Well I guess I paid for it. But I would have never thought to go to a place called Red State Barbecue and it was really good so.
(pause)
Yeah.
(pause)
Eh-hem.
(pause)
John
(pause)
John.
(pause)
JOHN YOU'RE BEING WEIRD TODAY JOHN.

JOHN   YEAH. YEAH I *AM* BEING WEIRD HIRO.

HIRO   Well stop! It was really awkward eating ribs in silence.

JOHN   Well I feel like if I'm not silent I'm just gonna start screaming!!!

HIRO   Why???

JOHN   Because I'm pissed!!!!!
(screaming out the window)
I'm PISSED off.

HIRO   At me!?!!?

JOHN   NO. I'm pissed because I'm STRESSED OUT
and feel useless as though my life has been for NOTHING.

HIRO   Oh God. Did something bad happen?

JOHN   No. Except for the fact that I spent the last
THIRTEEN YEARS OF MY FUCKING LIFE just
DEVOTED to my kid and he just doesn't do his FUCK-
ING HOMEWORK. EVEN THOUGH I DO EVERY-
THING FOR HIM. LITERALLY. EVERYTHING TO
MAKE HIS LIFE BETTER. And yesterday I was just
begging, pleading for him to stop doing this to me. To
just do his homework. And he's like okay cool, I'll do it.
And this morning, I checked his grades and his grades are
dropping because HE'S NOT DOING HIS HOME-
WORK. AND THEN LOOKED ON HIS BED AND
HE HAD LEFT THE HOMEWORK HE SAID HE
WAS GOING TO DO JUST, CRINKLED ON THE
BED UNDONE!!!! AND I JUST DON'T KNOW WHY
HE'S DOING THIS TO ME. WHAT DID I DO TO
DESERVE THIS? WHY JOHN JUNIOR. WHY.
WHYYYYY. WHYYYYYYYY. WHYYYYYYYYY.
WHYYYYY!!?!?!!!?!? WHYYYYYYYYYYY. SERIOUSLY.
WHYYYYYY? WHYYYYY?!!?!? WHYYYYY!!?!?

HIRO   You named your kid John Junior? Like after
yourself? That . . . takes a lot of gall—

JOHN   WHYYYYY?

An awkward pause.

HIRO   Um. Well. I don't have children. So.
   (pause)
   I don't really have anything to say.

They drive. JOHN *collects himself.*

JOHN   It just . . . makes me crazy you know? I'm
physically exhausting myself I'm so frustrated and angry.
And then I calm down and the adrenaline subsides and I
start shaking. More like shivering actually. See? I'm doing
it now.

JOHN *is shivering.* HIRO *looks at* JOHN *with a mixture of utter
disgust and mild concern.*

HIRO   . . . have you tried yoga?

JOHN   *What.*

JOHN *looks at* HIRO *with a mixture of utter disgust and mild
amusement.*

HIRO   Again. I do not have children. Nor do I ever plan
on having children. But I do know that having all that
anger just . . . living inside of you is bad.
   (pause)
   Do you see a therapist?

JOHN   What? No!

HIRO   Well. I have for years. And Larry really encour-
aged me to find a creative outlet. So outside of my work

I play music. I'm not very good but it doesn't matter. I
write little songs when I'm upset and just bang it out on
a banjo.

JOHN   A banjo? Ha. That's pretty cat.

HIRO   Cat?

JOHN   You don't remember we used to say that in high
school? That shit's cat. That's cat. You're cat?

HIRO   . . . absolutely not.

JOHN   Ah. Well all the cool kids said it.

HIRO   . . . Is being cat *good*?

JOHN   *It's cat.*
    (pause)
    Wanna sing me one of your songs?

HIRO   No! They're just for me. But that's the whole
point. You should find something that's just for you.

JOHN *stops the car.*

JOHN   Okay. Get out.

HIRO   Oh my God! I was just trying to be helpful
goddamnit. The ONE time I try to be helpful I get kicked
out of a fucking car in bum fuck—

JOHN   —shut up you fool I'm not mad I'm trying to
show you something!

HIRO   Show me what? Like your penis? Because I feel like that maybe that ship has sailed!

JOHN   JUST GET OUT OF MY FUCKING CAR.

HIRO *gets out of the car.* JOHN *also gets out. They stand side by side.* HIRO *has no idea what's going on. She watches* JOHN *look out into the distance—taking in a deep breath.* HIRO *doesn't know what to do.*

HIRO   What are you looking at?

JOHN   WHAT AM I LOOKING AT? Hiro are you serious??? I'm looking at that fucking picturesque piece of beautiful farmland right in front of us is what I'm looking at!

HIRO   What do you mean, "picturesque"?

JOHN   UM the gently rolling hills, sparsely wooded field complete with a little tiny creek running through it? THE FUCKING ADORABLE HORSE MOM WITH HER LITTLE PONY?

HIRO   'Kay.

JOHN   Anyway. You said I should find something that's just for me. Well—it's my dream to buy land like this someday. Just for me. Well. Me and my kid. So maybe moving forward when I'm angry I can come here or something. I dunno.

HIRO   Places like this give me anxiety.

JOHN   Why???

HIRO   It's too remote. And honestly, I'm having a hard time understanding why anyone would choose this. Sorry I don't mean to sound like "oh I'm a city mouse," and "you're a country mouse" but yeah. Can you . . . help me understand why this would be something you want?

JOHN   UGH DO YOU SERIOUSLY NEED ME TO MANSPLAIN THIS TO YOU?

HIRO   I WOULD LOVE THAT.

JOHN   OKAY. Well. For starters—many middle-class people's assets peak like in their fifties. And I know you lived in a shitty area—

HIRO   Hey now—

JOHN   —But I grew up solidly middle class. And in OUR economic class—

HIRO   —You're so condescending—

JOHN   —the kids move out and they downsize. But nobody has an estate anymore to pass down. When they retire, everyone just uses up everything they accumulated when they were younger and don't pass a lot on, and then the next middle-class generation has to work really fucking hard to catch up to their parents. It'd be nice to pass on some financial security to my kid.
   (pause)
   Legacy. Is something I think of a lot. And you know what? I'm smart. I have an MBA. This isn't an impossible dream. Wow. I already feel calmer.

HIRO   Oh my God.

JOHN   I know. I'm like a good parent. It's surprising.

HIRO   No I mean. Oh my God. What the fuck am I gonna do?

JOHN   Huh?

HIRO   *(freaking out)*
Like—what kind of fucking SHIT am I going to inherit when both of my parents fucking die which let's face it COULD BE SOON. My fucking dad doesn't think about shit like legacy! And my mom—FUCK. I DON'T EVEN THINK SHE HAS A FUCKING WILL. FUUUUUCK!!!!FUCCK!!!! FUUUUUCK. OH MY GOD FUUUUCK!!!!

JOHN   Um can you not freak out, I just literally talked myself out of a complete meltdown.

HIRO   AHH. AHHH. AHHHH. AND THEY HAVE ALL THIS DEBT. JOHN AM I GOING TO INHERIT THE DEBT? IS THAT HOW DEBT WORKS?

JOHN   I mean?

HIRO   AND THE HOUSE. OH GOD THE HOUSE. Sophie's been warning me this whole time and I've just been ignoring her! I'm so fucking stupid. JOHN. WHY AM I SO FUCKING STUPID? I HAVE TO GET MY SHIT TOGETHER. I HAVE TO CLEAN MY PAR-ENTS' HOUSE. JOHN WILL YOU DROP ME OFF THERE INSTEAD OF THE HOTEL?!?!

JOHN   Hey Hiro. It sounds like you just have some planning to do and it's still early—

HIRO   But it's not fucking early!!! Don't you get it?!!?
I'm running out of time. I fucked up. I fucked up John.
I'm running out of time!

Sound of MASAKO *crying again.*

This leads us to . . .

Scene Five

Hospital room, later that day. MASAKO *is crying in bed.* JAMES *watches her uncomfortably.*

JAMES Masako—you've been crying for an hour. It ain't gonna help nothin'.

MASAKO My bones hurt. I hate this medicine. It makes my bones go Muaaan muaaan.

JAMES There there.

JAMES *touches* MASAKO.

MASAKO *Don't touch me.*

JAMES Does it hurt when I touch ya?

MASAKO I don't want you to touch because *you* gave me cancer.

JAMES What now?

MASAKO You gave me cancer because you were so mean. You make me stressed out. You gave me cancer. This is your fault. This is your fault. Anata no sei! Anata no sei!!!!

MASAKO *starts hitting* JAMES. *He wants to shove her away or hit her back but he doesn't. He lets her hit him. We see this struggle. It's not easy.*

JAMES   Are you finished?

She's finished.

MASAKO   Not fair.

JAMES   *(a little more bitter and aggressive than he intended)*
   Nothing's fair.

MASAKO   *I know that. I'm not stupid. But this not fair mostly of all.* I take care of me. I eat smoothie. Drink almond milk. Vegetable. I drink wine only sometimes. And I walk five mile every day. And still I get sick. But you! You drink osake every day. Twenty pack of beer every day. You almost die. But now you fixed. It's not fair. I cannot see the light. I cannot see the light!

JAMES   Well of course you can't see the light Masako. *Because you are the light!*
   (pause)
   Okay?

MASAKO   . . . Okay.

JAMES   I'm just.
   (pause)
   I'm just glad you're as well as you are.

They hold hands. A few beats.

MASAKO   What did you do today.

JAMES   Flea Market.

MASAKO   Did you have fun?

JAMES   They call me the rock man over there cuz I'm a salesman of rocks. There was this guy in high school who used to carry around this big stick and he would pray about Jesus. They used to call him Stick Man. I'm like him but without God and with rocks.

MASAKO   There's God in you, James.

JAMES   Ya think?

MASAKO   I know. Because I used to pray all the time when you get mean. I was not religious but I pray anyway. And when Sophie became Christian she pray and I pray with her—please let James be the James I met in California again. Kawaii quiet James too pure for this world. He is shy. Hard for him to be sunao but when he does he is so cute. And it took many, many years but my prayer come true. No? That is why I believe now. In something a little more. I believe because of the God in you.

MASAKO *looks at* JAMES *a sweet moment. Fade to . . .*

Scene Six

HIRO. *Alone. She's on the phone.*

HIRO   So I wasn't planning on going back to my parents' house at all because it's filled with bad memories and I get so . . . triggered. Plus I'm a thirty-six-year-old account director with, like, assistants and everything. I can finally afford the hotel of my childhood dreams: the Hyatt Regency. But my mind really went into panic mode when you mentioned all that stuff about legacy. Everything hit me all at once.

Lights up on JOHN. HIRO *is on the phone with him.*

JOHN   Yeah sorry about that. I didn't mean to send you into a spiral. I just thought it was my turn to complain.

HIRO   So even before I walk in the door—the place is a fucking disaster. My dad has two cars in the driveway that don't even work plus a broken motorcycle. Nothing about the yard makes sense. Sticks everywhere. Dead trees. Dead flowers. An oddly blooming cherry tree. Yellow grass in the Bluegrass State.
   (pause)
   But then I go inside and . . . my shoulders soften. I'm breathing normally. And I feel . . . comfortable? Sure there's junk everywhere but I find myself kind of liking the junk? I mean what the fuck is that, becoming an adult? Liking the shit you used to hate?

73

JOHN   Sometimes things you hated in your childhood
can morph into feeling like an old relative. A crusty, dusty
part of your worn-down soul. God I'm tired.

HIRO   And I noticed something I had never seen before.
A photo of my mom and dad when they eloped, framed
and hanging proudly like it was meant to be there. Like
someone hung it.

JOHN   Why'd they elope? And how'd they even meet.
Your parents? Was your dad in the—

HIRO   No my father was not in the army you basic bitch.
Everyone asks me that. I know they met in California. I
don't know all the details. Never cared to ask.

JOHN   You should ask.

HIRO   Anyways—I started wondering . . . when was the
last time I saw my parents kiss? And I realized I never have
until this picture. So, I'm in my childhood home, with full
intention of throwing shit away and here I am staring at
my parents kissing for the first time ever in my life. *God.*
They looked so happy. And that's when it dawned on me that
there was a time before I was born when my parents were
just a couple. Independent of me. And Sophie. They were
just a couple in love. And then I did the dishes. And I
went back to the hospital.

JOHN   So you're not freaked out anymore?

HIRO   *(drily)* Of course I'm freaked out. The cycle of
poverty is an endless loop and I've deluded myself into
thinking I've escaped it. But that's what therapy, detox
cleanses, and Doo-Da are for.

JOHN   Da fuck's Doo-Da?

HIRO: My banjo. I don't know what's going to happen to my parents.

JOHN   That's just how it is.
(pause)
I think a lot of times parents just get caught in the bullshit like everybody else. I think about my dad and when he was young and . . . he was probably just caught up in bullshit too.

HIRO   . . . where are you right now?

JOHN   Home.

HIRO   I found some pot. Wanna smoke it with me? I can come over quick—

JOHN   I can't hang out tonight.

HIRO   Oh okay. One of your hoes coming over? Tammy Lynn or Chastity something?

JOHN   Naw. I'm hanging out with John Jr. We're gonna watch a movie.
(pause)
He crashed his bicycle today.

HIRO   Oh no! Is he okay?

JOHN   Yeah just a little banged up. But he was crying. And it hurts me so bad when he cries. God, I love him so much.

HIRO   Do you tell him that?

JOHN   Every fucking day.

HIRO   He's lucky. I've never heard my dad say, "I Love You."

JOHN   Well, you know what Hiro? My dad never said it either. But I know he did. That's something I learned when I became a parent. Even when you can't express it, you are always, *always* overwhelmed with love for your kid. *God you'd do anything to protect them.* I'm so broken today because John Jr. fell off his bike. I wish I was there to catch him.
  (pause)
  Shit I gotta go. *Transformers* is starting.

HIRO   Alright.

JOHN   *(toward his son)*
  Be right there bug!
  (pause)
  Bye Hiro.

HIRO   Bye John.

HIRO *alone again. She rolls a joint, or whatever weed contraption is convenient. She takes a drag.* SOPHIE *enters.*

HIRO   Soph what are you doing here? It's not your shift is it? Did I fuck up?

SOPHIE   No. Da'Ran's having a bro night and I just wanted to be with Mama.

HIRO   And what does "bro night" look like for Da'Ran.

SOPHIE   Sober poker. Church basement. They play with chips.

(pause)

Are you seriously smoking weed in a hospital parking lot?

HIRO   Get this. It's Dad's. His stash was just sitting right there on his nightstand next to an Elvis statue and a mountain of rocks so I took it!

SOPHIE   You went to the house. What a mess, right?

HIRO *nods.*

SOPHIE   Did I tell you Dad still smoked when he was trying to get on the transplant list?

HIRO   Is that allowed??

SOPHIE   Heck no. It's hard for an alcoholic to get on a transplant list in the first place. Gotta go to AA. All that. Prove they're clean—

HIRO   Well he *did* get sober—

SOPHIE   But he still smoked. And when he got through a month of sobriety so that he could get on the transplant list the doctors were like . . . Mr. Rose . . . you tested positive for marijuana we can't put you on the list. And he was like HUHHHHHHHH?!?!?!

HIRO   What a dumbass!

SOPHIE   So he quit smoking for like a month. Got put on the list. But then boom! He magically doesn't need a transplant anymore. So he started smoking again.

HIRO   Livers are so weird.

SOPHIE   It's a miracle. I wonder why Dad got a miracle but Mama didn't.

HIRO   She still might.

A pause.

SOPHIE   It's been hard not to lose hope.

HIRO   But you've always been so hopeful.

SOPHIE   Hiro, I can't. I can't have children.

HIRO   . . . What?

SOPHIE   I have PCOS. It can make it difficult to get pregnant sometimes but I found out about a month ago that I can't ovulate. You haven't had anything similar?

HIRO *shakes her head no.*

SOPHIE   You've never had any problems? Like ever?

HIRO *hasn't.* SOPHIE *gets upset.*

SOPHIE   I wanted me and Da'Ran's children more than anything else in the world.

HIRO   You can adopt! They'll still be your children.

SOPHIE   I know. I know. But I really wanted to be pregnant. I wanted Mama to touch my pregnant belly and make little blankets and hats and—

HIRO   She can still make blankets. She can still—

SOPHIE   *I know you don't want kids. You've always talked about it. Why don't you want kids?*

HIRO   Because I don't want to end up like Dad.

SOPHIE   We're not our parents! I would have been amazing—

HIRO   And I know that and you still will be, but I don't wanna risk it. I'm so sorry Sophie. I wish I could give you my ovaries. I wish I could give you my ovaries and Dad could give mom his immortality.

HIRO *goes to comfort* SOPHIE. SOPHIE *is comforted. A beat.*
HIRO *offers* SOPHIE *a puff of her joint (or whatever contraption works best).*

HIRO   Want some?
   (pause)
   Just kidding. I know you don't.

SOPHIE   Sure.

HIRO   What?

SOPHIE   I said sure. I'll take a hit. F it. God will still love me.

HIRO *passes a joint to* SOPHIE *with utter glee. She's smoking pot with her sister for the first time!!!!!!! Yeee!!!* SOPHIE *takes a hit. She doesn't cough or anything.*

She takes another one, then takes a deep breath.

HIRO   You're *good* at that.

SOPHIE   I used to be wild before Jesus found me, Hiro.
Woke up once half-naked on the roof of Rock Haven
looking up at the morning stars . . .

HIRO   Rock Haven? The eighteen and under club!?!?!!
Hahahaaaa—

SOPHIE   It was a school night. And I thought I was
soooo cat.

She takes another hit. Passes it to HIRO.

HIRO   I wish we would have hung out more when you
were wild.

SOPHIE   You were in New York by then. I think that's
part of what made me so wild. I was lonely.

HIRO   Thanks for telling me that.
    (pause)
I'm afraid Mom will die. And I didn't get to tell her all
the things I needed to tell her.

SOPHIE   Me too.

HIRO   But I don't even know what I need to tell her,
you know? I already feel normal. Her changing body. Her
vomiting in front of me. It doesn't traumatize me.

SOPHIE   Well, it traumatizes me. It's my mama.

HIRO   But Soph.
    (pause)
When Mom would cry and cry and cry in bed because

Dad would rage at her for doing something that wasn't
even remotely wrong like turning the heat up so we'd be
warm and she'd lay in the middle of us and we'd sandwich
her and pat her head so that she could go muster up the
strength to go apologize to him and say "Sorry sorry
James. I'm sorry I was wrong please forgive me," and
afterwards we would be like "Yaaay good job mom!" . . .
was that traumatizing for you?

SOPHIE   No that was normal.

HIRO   See. I'm still traumatized by that. And this is why
I can't forgive him. But Sophie. I need to forgive him. I
need to forgive Dad for the sake of Mom in these mo-
ments. To give her peace. And I know that. But I can't.
How did you do it?

SOPHIE   It wasn't easy. That's all I can say is that it
wasn't easy. God—

HIRO   Don't tell me it was God.
   (*pause*)
Sorry. It's just.
   (*pause*)
Sophie, did I tell you that I went to church?

SOPHIE   *You?*

HIRO   St. John The Divine. It's a Cathedral up by
Columbia.

SOPHIE   What for the decorations or—

HIRO   Because I was lost.

SOPHIE   Like literally lost or?

HIRO   No. Because I was *feeling* lost.

SOPHIE *laughs.* HIRO *is serious.*

SOPHIE   OH wait. You're serious. Sorry I'm like super-
high and this is like. Blowing my mind right now. Go on.

HIRO   And I walked in and . . .

SOPHIE   *And . . . ?*

HIRO   Security was like. Sorry ma'am we're closing.

SOPHIE *laughs more.*

HIRO   But I think I wanted to feel close to God so I
went to church. And I don't know God. But you know
God. And I wanted to be close to you. I've lost too much
time with you because I was so angry. I lost time with
Mom too.

SOPHIE   But you had every right. Every right to be
angry.
    (pause)
    Hey, you wanna know besides God—how I learned to
forgive Dad?

HIRO   Yes.

SOPHIE   I forgave him by paying attention to his
language of love.
    (pause; this means everything to HIRO*)*
    People have different ways of loving. And Dad can't
love with his words. Most of the time. But he shows a lot
of love and remorse through his actions.

HIRO   How?

SOPHIE   What would he always do after a blind drunken rage? How would we know the storm was over?

HIRO   He'd go to the store.

SOPHIE   And what would he always say when he was on his way to the store?

HIRO   "I'm going to Kroger. Want me to pick you up anything?"

SOPHIE   That was him saying "I'm sorry."

HIRO   And we'd say no.

SOPHIE   But he'd bring us each a candy bar anyway.

HIRO   *(a realization)*
And that was him saying "I love you."

Scene Seven

A little later. Hospital. Same. JAMES *is singing Dan Hill's hit song "Sometimes When We Touch" softly to* MASAKO *in bed.*

JAMES   *(singing)*
  And who am I to judge you
  In what you say or do
  I'm only just beginning
  To see the real you
  And sometimes when we touch
  The honesty's too much
  And I have to close my eyes
  And hide
  I want to hold you 'til I die
  'Til we both break down and cry
  I want to hold you 'til the fear in me subsides

SOPHIE *and* HIRO *enter; they are hiiiigh.*

HIRO   Woah woah woah woah woah whaaaaaat is going on here???

SOPHIE   I feel like I just caught you two having sex. Oh my gosh do you remember when I actually caught you having sex? I heard screaming coming from your room and I hadn't ever seen y'all kiss so I thought someone was murdering Mama so I rolled in with my huge US history book to beat the burglars away and caught you rolling naked off of Dad!!!!!

MASAKO   Ohhh yes. I remember.

HIRO   Hahhahahahahahahaha whaaat. That did NOT happen.

SOPHIE   Oh my gooooshhh I think that was a repressed memory!!!

HIRO   I didn't know you guys had sex. I've never even seen you kiss in person.

SOPHIE   Why didn't anyone ever talk to me about that?

HIRO   You guys should kiss *now*. Kiss! Kiss! Kiss! Kiss! Kiss! Kiss! Kiss!!!

SOPHIE   Yeah kiss!!!!!

HIRO   Kiss!!!!!

JAMES   What the hell are you guys on?

SOPHIE   YOUUUUUUUR DRUGS!!!!!!

HIRO   I STOLE YOUR STASH. Oh my god I told him. I actually told him!!!!

JAMES   My stash? You done stole my stash?!?!? Well I'll be.

JAMES *is laughing.* MASAKO *is laughing too.*

SOPHIE   MAMA. YOU LOOK SO MUCH BETTER.

MASAKO   I am feeling better.

JAMES   Chemo's done. She's just on potassium now.

MASAKO   Potassium like banana!

SOPHIE *and* HIRO *celebrate vocally.* MASAKO *joins in.*

JAMES   So we got a choice. Doctors say if she finishes the paperwork she can leave around midnight. Or we can wait 'til the morning.

SOPHIE   What do you wanna do Mama?

HIRO   Yeah what do you wanna do? If you wanna go home tonight me and Sophie can wait!

SOPHIE   Yeah lets wait!!!!!

MASAKO   Yaaaay!

SOPHIE/HIRO   YAAAAAAY!

HIRO   *(looking at her dad)* You can stay too.
   (pause)
   If you want.

JAMES   . . . okay.

MASAKO   Yaaaaay. I'm so happy!!!!

Squealing. Celebrating. Then the excitement dies down. Stillness. Quiet that goes on for a while. JAMES *then starts playing around on his phone.*

HIRO   So do you like. Wanna tell us the story of how you two met?

MASAKO   Why?

JAMES   I'm busy.

HIRO   Busy with what?

JAMES   I'm chatting with my rock friends on Facebook.

SOPHIE   What do you guys talk about?

JAMES   Rocks.

Another beat. And then.

SOPHIE   Daad . . . Mom . . . Dad . . . Dadd . . .

JAMES   WHAT.

SOPHIE   Why do you live in Kentucky? You guys met in California. Why did you raise us in Kentucky? I mean I love it here don't get me wrong but why?

HIRO   Yeah California has so many Asians.

MASAKO   Kentucky has Asian. I teach piano only to Asian girls and boys. I make living.

SOPHIE   But why Kentucky.

JAMES   What is with all these questions?

HIRO   Just tell us!

SOPHIE   Yeah tell us.

JAMES   Well. Kentucky is where your Grandma and Grandpa was. And that's where I was from. So figured we'd go back.

HIRO   Is that it?

JAMES   Yup.

Another long pause. SOPHIE *and* HIRO *are mystified. This is the first time this family has had an honest conversation in a while.*

SOPHIE   Dad. Daaaad.

JAMES   WHAT?

SOPHIE   When you go to the Chinoe pub for karaoke every night do you buy anything?

JAMES   I give them a dollar for the water and I give them a dollar when I sing.

HIRO   I'm surprised they let you in.

JAMES   The owner is my friend.

HIRO   You have friends?

MASAKO   He has many friends. And I have many friends too. My best friend name is Chip. James best friend name Morino san and he call him Mr. Trees.
   (SOPHIE *laughs with her mom;* MASAKO *looks at* HIRO)
That nickname is bilingual double entendre. You would not understand.

JAMES   He told the bartender not to serve me beer.

HIRO   Why would you ask for beer when you know you'd die if you drink it?

JAMES   I don't ask for beer. Sometimes people try to buy it for me because of my great singing. But the bartender knows not to let 'em.

HIRO   Well you had enough beer to last you a lifetime.

JAMES   Hmmm.

MASAKO   Hiro be nice to your father he work very hard.

SOPHIE   Mama what did you want to be when you grew up?

MASAKO   A mother.

A nice beat.

SOPHIE   Dad how about you?

JAMES   I didn't really think about it. I was too busy riding horses. Playing sports.

HIRO   Do you regret not thinking about it?

JAMES   No, *Miss Account Director.*

SOPHIE   *(cracking herself up)* With like assistants and everything!

JAMES   I'm having a nice ride. I meet a lot of people. Talk about whatever I want.
   (pause)
   When I was nineteen, I started studying business but stopped because it was so boring.

MASAKO   He's very smart.

JAMES   So I traveled with nothing in my pockets 'cept for a dime.
   (pause)
   You spend a lot of time at work. But if you're not interested in what you're doing with your work—your life is gonna be hell. A lot of people never figure out what they're living for. They just do stuff to stay alive. That's the world as it is.

HIRO   Did you like working overnights at Sam's Club before being on disability?

JAMES   As a matter of fact, yes. Yes I did.

MASAKO   . . . I miss you.

Everyone looks at MASAKO.

SOPHIE   What was that, Mama?

MASAKO   I was just thinking girls. How I had bad time. So, so bad laying here. But now good thing happened. And that is feeling our family together. Like Christmas and birthday. Better than Christmas and birthday. But I miss you. And I think—how can I miss someone who is here? But I think that's because . . . the more I'm around you the more I wish I knew you as much as you knew yourself. The more I wish I could protect you more than you can protect yourself. Ever since you were born I just wanted to protect you. And now you protect me. I am so lucky. I am so, so lucky. I'm so lucky *cancer is over. It's over!!!!* Oh I'm so lucky you are here. Oh I'm so lucky I get to miss you in this moment.

SOPHIE   We're right here, Mama, we're right here.

SOPHIE *goes to her mom and hugs her.* HIRO *follows. They sandwich her in a group hug.* JAMES *doesn't join in, instead he looks on as the prelude to Dan Hill's "Sometimes When We Touch" plays over the speakers.*

HIRO, MASAKO, *and* SOPHIE *freeze in a tableau as the lights fade into a BLACKOUT. The song keeps playing in the dark. We listen to a lot of it. Through the scene change and a bit into the next scene until . . .*

Scene Eight

JAMES, *alone.*

JAMES   Hi. I'm James. And I'm a . . .
(pause)
I'm an alcoholic.
(pause)
I see a lot of you in here today that I've become . . .
friends with.
Sorry. Words can be hard.
(pause)
Oh! My daughters. They asked me how me and my wife
met. And. At the time. I didn't feel like getting into it. But
I guess now is the appropriate time to get into it.
(pause)
I saw Masako before I met her. About seven times to be
exact. And for seven days I couldn't talk to her. Because
she was just so damn . . .
(pause)
See, it was the seventies and I had hitchhiked from
Kentucky to Berkeley and was livin' outside because it was
warm. And I like the earth. I showered at the port. I was
clean and I was happy. And one sunny day I noticed this
woman, sitting on a bench nearby my tent. This dark-
haired, tiny woman and I thought to myself . . . that is
one . . .
(pause)
So naturally I couldn't go talk to her. And I watched
her go. And kicked myself in the damn nuts. But lo and

behold . . . the next day she came back and sat down with
a book! *War and Peace*. So I knew she was smart, too.
Which scared me even more. I thought about starting up
a conversation but I hadn't read *War and Peace* ever in
my life so. I watched her go again, knowing she was out
of my . . .
   (pause)
   But then the next day goddamnit there she was again!
Holding flowers this time. Tulips to be exact. Purple, pink,
and gold. And I thought—this is it, James. You gotta go
talk to this woman. But fuck! Some other dipshit got to
her first. Sat down right next to her and started strikin' up
a conversation. He had long hair. Mustache. Looked like
his name would be "Sandy" or "Sky"—you know the type.
So I retreated. And the next day it rained and the mood of
the sky matched my damn heart. And I sat there sulking
lookin' at the clouds until . . . right there on that bench
again . . . there she was. Holding an umbrella—looking at
the clouds too! I couldn't believe it! But . . . when I took
two steps forward I took two steps back cause I saw that
she was . . . crying. Not the way I learned Masako could
cry and cry and cry 'til you wanted her to shut up but just
a soft type of crying like in a painting or somethin' so I left
her alone. And besides there was this voice inside of me
right then. A voice inside of me that said—it's okay to
leave her alone. Because she'll be back tomorrow. And the
next day she was back. But she still seemed sad. I figured
that fucker Sandy, Skyler, or whatever—he probably did
something. Figured she needs some space she needs some
more time.
   She needs more time.
   So on the sixth day when she came—I still didn't
approach—but I promised that on the seventh—on the
seventh day I'd talk to her. And she was wearing this beautiful yellow dress on that seventh day.

MASAKO *enters. She is wearing a yellow dress.*

JAMES   And she looked like herself again. So before she could sit down on that bench I marched right on up to her and said, Hi. I'm James. James Rose.

MASAKO   I'm Masako Shiota.

JAMES   It's nice to meet you.

MASAKO   It's nice to meet you, too.

JAMES   And I asked her what she was doing right now and she said—

MASAKO   I am visiting America for first time. I am lonely but I am happy. This is my favorite place to come and sit. Think about my life.

JAMES   And she asked me—

MASAKO   What are you doing now?

JAMES   And for some reason I told her I was on my way to the record store.

MASAKO   Oh?

JAMES   I didn't want her to think I was a stalker even though I kinda was I suppose but I said, Yes. I am on my way to the record store to buy a record.

MASAKO   Which record?

JAMES   And the first song that came to my mind was— this song we just played for you.

MASAKO   "Sometimes When We Touch," by Dan Hill?
That song I love!!!!

JAMES   You do?

MASAKO   Yes! Yes!
(singing)
And sometimes when we touch
The honesty's too much
(speaking)
So romantic!!!!

JAMES   And I mustered up the rest of my courage and
asked . . . Would you like to come with me? To the record
store?

MASAKO   Yes James. I would love to come with you to
the record store.

JAMES   And off we went. And we held hands. And we
held each other. And we spoke things like—

MASAKO   Suki. I like you.

JAMES   Suki too. And—

MASAKO   Ai shiteru. I love you.

JAMES   And—

MASAKO   OH NO JAMES I'M GETTING
DEPORTED.

JAMES   NO YOU FUCKING AIN'T MASAKO—
MARRY ME.

MASAKO   I do!

JAMES   I do.

MASAKO   'Til death do us part.

HIRO *enters. She's wearing black.*

JAMES   And she said things like . . .

MASAKO   I want children.

SOPHIE *enters. She's wearing black too.*

MASAKO   I know I'd be a good mother, James.

SOPHIE, HIRO, *and* JAMES *all stand side by side. We realize now that* JAMES *is wearing a black blazer or jacket.*

MASAKO   And you. You would be a *good* father.

JAMES   Masako and I. We've had our up and downs but we were married thirty-seven years and she was the strongest woman I'd ever met. I mean she married me didn't she? And stayed married to me until the day she died. I think . . . I think sometimes I was hard on her because I knew she could take it.
    And she was a fighter. Even when the cancer kept comin' back and parts of her body gave out she kept on like she was whole. And when she couldn't stand anymore . . . she stood. She even played the damn piano. I don't know if she ever knew she was dying because she was so full of life.
    (pause)
    I say. I say. Masako's strength went unnoticed sometimes. A lot of people thought she was weak because she was cute and small and she was nice and she smiled a lot but it takes a lot of strength to smile. It does. It takes a lot

of strength to be nice. Being an asshole is easy. If my wife taught me anything it's the courage to be . . . patient and kind. And I promise I will try to live patiently and kindly for her. And goddamnit I will try to smile more.

MASAKO *is gone now.*

JAMES   Anyway I don't know what else to say I've never had to give no eulogy before.
   (realizing he forgot something)
   OH FUCK!!!!

He takes out a crinkled piece of paper.

JAMES   I forgot . . . I forgot the shit I wrote down.

JAMES *reads from the crinkled paper.*

JAMES   *(full conviction)* MASAKO LIKED THE OCEAN. AND SHE APPRECIATED JUDGE JUDY. OKAY. Okay I'm done. That's it. I'm done. Whew I'm finished. I'm finished. I'm fucking finished. I'm finished.

He takes a deep breath. A beat as HIRO, SOPHIE, *and* JAMES *look out.*

HIRO   Well what the fuck do we do now?

SOPHIE *is too devastated to talk. Another beat.*

JAMES   Well.
   (pause)
   I was thinkin' about rushing off to Kroger to pick up some things. Who knows when we'll get to eating—talking to all these damned people.
   (pause)
   Want me to get you something? Like a candy bar?

A beat.

HIRO   . . . yes.

SOPHIE   Yes.

JAMES   . . . Yes????
   (pause)
   Alright then. Off I go.

END OF PLAY